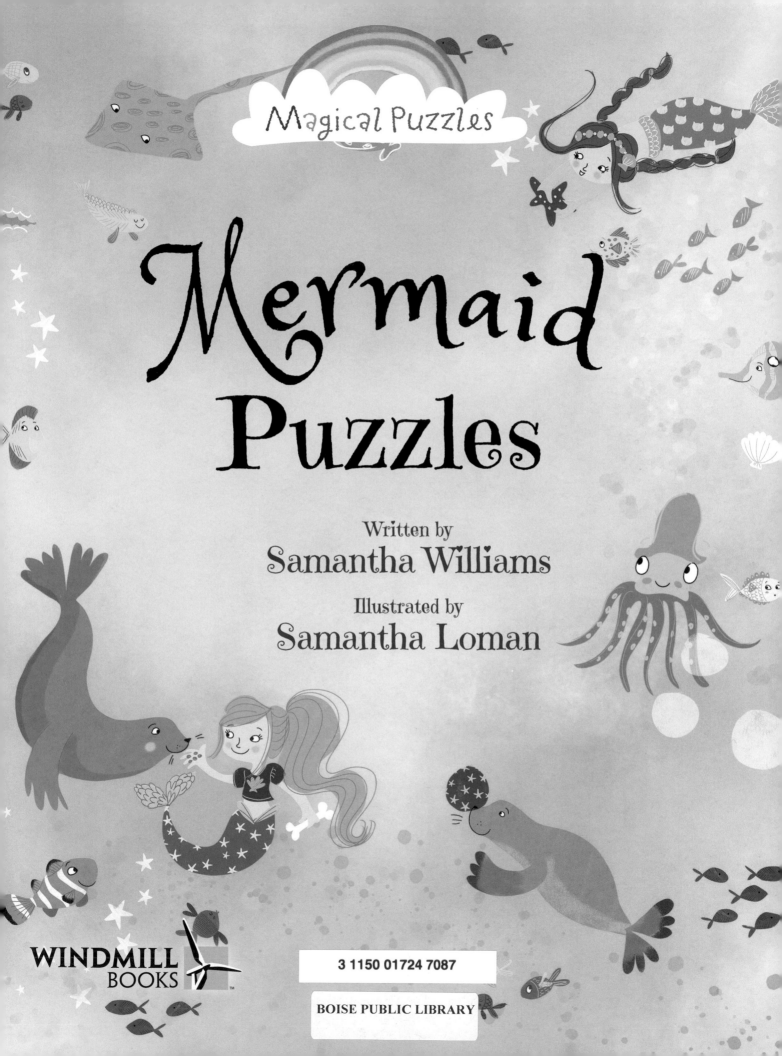

Magical Puzzles

Mermaid Puzzles

Written by
Samantha Williams

Illustrated by
Samantha Loman

WINDMILL BOOKS

Published in 2020 by **Windmill Books**, an imprint of Rosen Publishing
29 East 21st Street, New York, NY 10010

Copyright © Arcturus Holdings Limited

Illustrated by Samantha Loman
Written by Samantha Williams
Edited by Susannah Bailey
Designed by Well Nice Ltd

Cataloging-in-Publication Data

Names: Williams, Samantha. | Loman, Sam.
Title: Mermaid puzzles / Samantha Williams, illustrated by Sam Loman.
Description: New York : Windmill Books, 2020. | Series: Magical puzzles
Identifiers: ISBN 9781538391808 (pbk.) | ISBN 9781538391822 (library bound)
| ISBN 9781538391815 (6 pack)
Subjects: LCSH: Picture puzzles--Juvenile literature. | Mermaids--Juvenile literature.
Classification: LCC GV1507.P47 W55 2020 | DDC 793.73--dc23

Manufactured in the United States of America

CPSIA Compliance Information: Batch #BS19WM:
For Further Information contact Rosen Publishing, New York, New York at 1-800-237-9932

Contents

Say Hello!

Unscramble the letters to find out the names of these four friendly mermaids.

ORCAL

AREPL

HYLELS

QAUA

A

B

C

D

Under the Sea

Welcome to the mermaids' watery world!
Can you spot the items shown below?

Gift Giving

Aqua is making a necklace for her friend, Pearl. Study the pattern, and figure out which two shells she needs to thread onto the end.

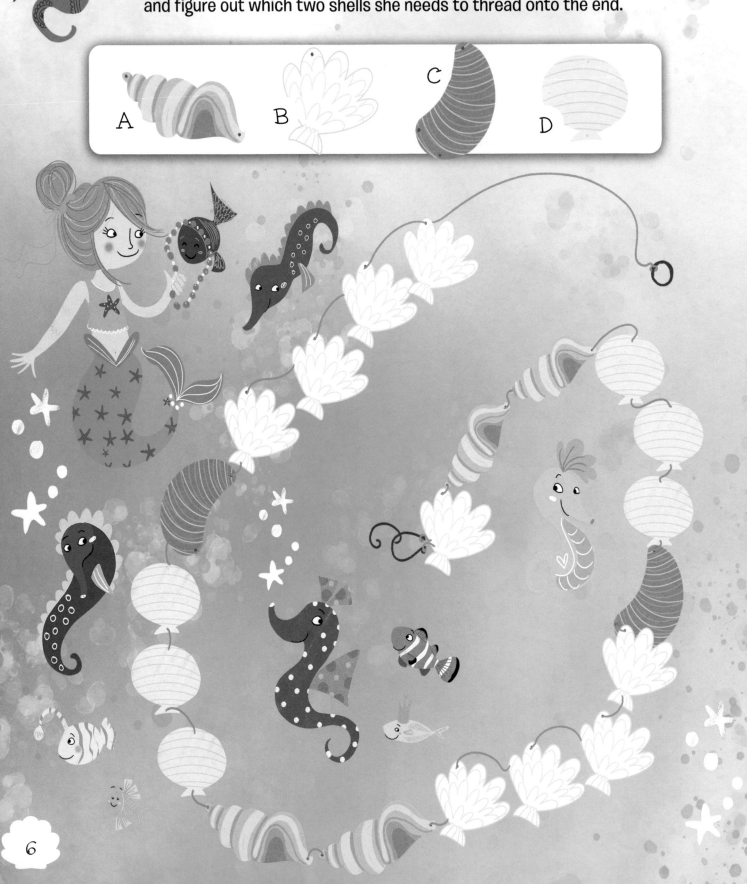

A   B   C   D

Secret Message

Copy this grid onto a piece of paper, then fill in all the boxes that contain the letters S, E, and A. The remaining letters spell a message from Coral and Shelly.

E	S	A	S	S	A	E	E	S	A
A	E	S	E	E	S	E	A	A	E
S	E	S	J	E	O	A	I	E	N
A	E	E	E	S	A	S	E	A	S
E	S	O	S	U	E	R	S	A	S
A	E	A	E	A	S	A	S	E	E
E	S	E	E	S	A	S	A	E	S
S	A	S	F	A	U	A	N	A	E
S	S	E	A	S	A	S	E	A	S
E	E	A	S	A	A	E	A	S	A

7

What's Your Mermaid Name?

Answer the questions and follow the arrows to find out!

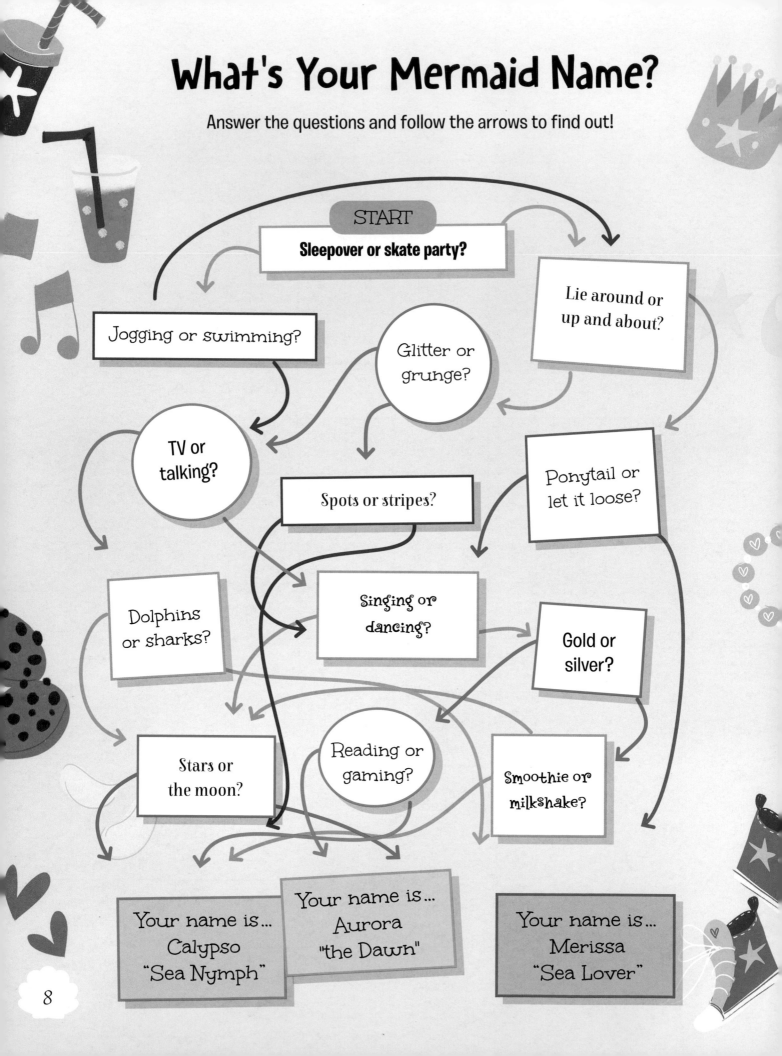

START
Sleepover or skate party?

Lie around or up and about?

Jogging or swimming?

Glitter or grunge?

TV or talking?

Ponytail or let it loose?

Spots or stripes?

Dolphins or sharks?

Singing or dancing?

Gold or silver?

Stars or the moon?

Reading or gaming?

Smoothie or milkshake?

Your name is...
Calypso
"Sea Nymph"

Your name is...
Aurora
"the Dawn"

Your name is...
Merissa
"Sea Lover"

8

Stormy Seas

Take a look at these two pictures, and try to spot eight differences between them.

Seeing Stars

The mermaids are star-hunting in this shipwreck scene.
How many are there? Remember to look for all types of stars!

Magical Mer-king

Which of the jigsaw pieces below completes the royal scene?

A B C D

Undersea Creatures

Can you find these swimming sea creatures hidden in the grid?
Words can be found forward, backward, and diagonally.

CRAB

OCTOPUS

FISH

DOLPHIN

S	E	A	N	O	I	L	A	E	S
S	D	O	L	P	H	I	N	S	F
H	E	W	E	R	P	N	C	R	I
E	C	A	T	H	C	A	E	C	S
L	A	R	H	P	R	B	A	U	H
A	B	S	A	O	T	E	U	C	B
H	S	O	L	B	R	L	S	O	O
W	R	P	L	O	B	S	T	E	R
P	R	T	S	W	L	S	E	P	O
S	U	P	O	T	C	O	T	S	B

SEAHORSE

WHALE

SEA LION

LOBSTER

Golden Bells and Pearl Shells

Welcome to the royal palace! How many golden bells and pearl shells can you count in this picture?

BELL

SHELL

15

Wavy Hair!

Pearl is washing her beautiful, long curls. Which of her shadows exactly matches the main picture?

Mer-maze

Can you help Coral avoid the eels on her way back to the palace?

17

Starry Night

Shelly loves to swim to the surface at night and gaze at the stars.
Can you spot this constellation?

Seadoku

Copy the grid below onto a separate piece of paper. Use the pictures above the grid to fill in the blank spaces, making sure that each line across, each line down, and each mini grid has just one of each picture.

Mermaid Song

Can you find a musical note that appears only once on this page?

Odd Otter Out

Which of these sea otters looks slightly different?

Mer-map

Use the grid on the map to answer the questions.
For example, the turtles are in square 2B.

Write your answers on a separate piece of paper.

1. Look at square 4C. How many mermaids are there?

2. Find squares 5B, 5C, and 5D. Where is the octopus?

3. Is there a whale or a shark in 2E?

4. Which letter is on the row where the dolphins play?

5. Which square contains the Mer-king: 3A, 2E, or 4B?

6. What creature is in 3A?

7. If you want to visit the palace, should you go to 1B?

8. Which column has the most mermaids in it: 1, 3, or 4?

Mermaid Whispers

It's so much fun playing games with your friends!
For this one, you'll need at least four of you, sitting in a line.

The person at one end (let's imagine it is you) thinks of something silly to say.
Try something like:

"Many of the mermaids get the giggles when they gossip."

Whisper it to the person sitting next to you. That person then whispers the message to the next person, but it has to be done immediately, with no thinking time, and you can only hear the message once.

Work to the end of the line, passing the message on quickly. There is a big chance that the message you end up with won't be anything like the original!

Tangled Tiaras

Oops! Aqua has gotten her tiaras in a big muddle.
Can you count how many there are on the page?

Find the Friends

The mermaids have lots of creatures to play with under the sea.
Look at the list, and then find all of them in the picture.

pink octopus

merboy

crab

clownfish

turtle

lobster

sea snail

blacktip shark

Ring, Ring!

Which of these beautiful gems does Shelly find in her treasure box?
Use the clues to work it out.

1. It contains at least one red stone.

2. It doesn't have any green stones on it.

3. It has three stones on it.

4. It contains at least one pink stone.

5. It doesn't have any blue stones.

Bubble Trouble

Find a way through the bubble maze to get to Casey the crab.

START

FINISH

Answers

Page 4: Say Hello!
A Coral, B Pearl, C Aqua, D Shelly

Page 5: Under the Sea

Page 6: Gift Giving
A, A

Page 7: Secret Message
JOIN OUR FUN

Page 9: Stormy Seas

Pages 10: Seeing Stars
28

Page 12: Magical Mer-king
D

Page 13: Undersea Creatures

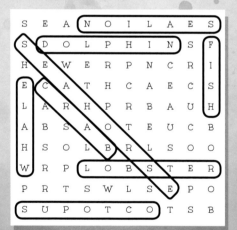

S	E	A	N	O	I	L	A	E	S
S	D	O	L	P	H	I	N	S	F
H	E	W	E	R	P	N	C	R	I
E	C	A	T	H	C	A	E	C	S
L	A	R	H	P	R	B	A	U	H
A	B	S	A	O	T	E	U	C	B
H	S	O	L	B	R	L	S	O	O
W	R	P	L	O	B	S	T	E	R
P	R	T	S	W	L	S	E	P	O
S	U	P	O	T	C	O	T	S	B

Pages 14: Golden Bells and Pearl Shells
Golden bells: 7. Pearl shells: 14.

Page 16: Wavy Hair
C

Page 17: Mer-maze

Page 18: Starry Night

Page 19: Seadoku

Page 20: Mermaid Song

Page 21: Odd Otter Out
C - the tail is curling a different way.

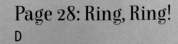

Pages 22: Mer-map

1   2
2   5C
3   A whale
4   A
5   4B
6   A whale
7   No, 4B and 5B
8   Column 1

Page 25: Tangled Tiaras

12

Pages 26:
Find the Friends

Page 28: Ring, Ring!

D

Page 29: Bubble Trouble

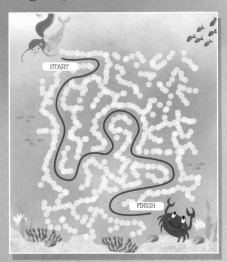